Original title:
Faint Whispers

Copyright © 2024 Swan Charm
All rights reserved.

Author: Mirell Mesipuu
ISBN HARDBACK: 978-9908-1-2710-1
ISBN PAPERBACK: 978-9908-1-2711-8
ISBN EBOOK: 978-9908-1-2712-5

Lullabies of Lost Moments

In the hush of fading light,
Whispers dance like fireflies bright.
Memories linger, soft and sweet,
Time drifts slowly, bittersweet.

Echoes of laughter still resound,
In corners where love was found.
Each sigh a gentle kiss of fate,
We hold each moment, contemplate.

Stars blink down from velvet skies,
Carrying secrets in their sighs.
Dreams entwined in silken night,
We cradle them till morning light.

Tears fall softly like the rain,
Each drop a note in silent pain.
But hope shines bright through shadows deep,
In lullabies we dare to keep.

So close your eyes and drift away,
To places where the heart can play.
In slumber's arms, find solace true,
In lost moments, I wait for you.

The Language of Solitude

In stillness, voices softly weave,
Threads of silence, souls believe.
Words unheard, yet deeply felt,
A tapestry of hearts that melt.

Shadows whisper in the dark,
In solitude, we leave our mark.
Embracing what the world denies,
In quietude, our spirit flies.

A single tear can speak for years,
Echoing our silent fears.
Tangled thoughts, a quiet storm,
In solitude, we find our form.

The moon reflects our hidden scars,
A language spoken between stars.
In the whispers of the night,
We gather strength to seek the light.

Though alone, we are not lost,
In silence, we embrace the cost.
Each moment savored, every breath,
In solitude, we conquer death.

Silent Conversations

Beneath the surface, feelings flow,
Expressions hidden, soft and slow.
A glance exchanged, a fleeting spark,
In silence speaks a truth, so stark.

Fingers brush on paths unseen,
In quietude, a shared routine.
Every pause, a tender space,
In silent talks, we find our grace.

Sighs intertwine with the evening breeze,
An understanding that brings us ease.
In every heartbeat, worlds collide,
Silent conversations, hearts confide.

No need for words, our souls engage,
Stories written page by page.
In the stillness, love takes flight,
Together, we ignite the night.

In shadows deep, our secrets bloom,
In softest whispers, there's no room.
For all the chaos life can bring,
Silent conversations set us free.

Gravity of Unspoken Words

In the space where thoughts collide,
Weight of silence often hides.
Words unsaid, a heavy load,
In the heart, they find their road.

A glance can hold a thousand tales,
While stillness breathes, the meaning swells.
In stuffy air, what's left unvoiced,
Becomes the choice that leaves us lost.

Like shadows cast in fading light,
Unspoken words take silent flight.
Each missed chance, a quiet plea,
In longing eyes, we seek to see.

Hearts confide in muted cries,
The truth lives beneath the lies.
In every sigh, a story waits,
Gravity binds our heavy fates.

Yet hope persists through cloudy skies,
With every breath, a new sunrise.
In the silence, we begin to learn,
To give those words a chance to turn.

Ethereal Whispers of the Cosmos

In the dark embrace of night,
Stars whisper tales of time,
Galaxies swirl in gentle flight,
Woven in a cosmic rhyme.

Nebulas bloom like flowers,
Unfolding secrets bright,
Every hour, an ancient power,
Guiding us through endless light.

Planets dance in silent grace,
Orbits trace a perfect line,
In this vast, ethereal space,
All our dreams intertwine.

Comets streak with fleeting glow,
Chasing shadows through the sky,
In their wake, a spark to show,
Where our heart's desires lie.

Whispers drift on cosmic winds,
Echoes of what's yet to be,
In the stillness, wisdom spins,
Revealing truths, wild and free.

Resonance of the Unseen

Beneath the surface, currents flow,
Hidden forces move with grace,
Whispers of what we may not know,
In shadows, dreams find their place.

A heartbeat echoes through the dark,
Silent paths of fate align,
Connecting souls, igniting a spark,
Reveal the ties that intertwine.

In the quiet, soft vibrations hum,
Songs of realms that lie beyond,
Through subtle hints, the answers come,
In every moment, we respond.

We sense the pull, a lingering thread,
Linking thoughts that float like mist,
In a tapestry of dreams we've spread,
Embracing all that we can't resist.

With each breath, the unseen weaves,
A symphony of hearts aligned,
In resonance, the world believes,
A dance of souls, forever entangled.

Echoes of a Forgotten Promise

Once a vow whispered in the breeze,
Soft as petals on the ground,
Time has worn it like the trees,
Yet in dreams, it still resounds.

In shadows cast by fading light,
Memories linger, bittersweet,
Holding on with all their might,
Binding hearts that yearn to meet.

Pages turn in silent books,
A tale of love lost in time,
Yet in the echoes, one still looks,
For the promise, pure and prime.

Through the silence, soft and clear,
Voices call from far away,
Guiding us to face our fears,
Reminding us of yesterday.

In twilight's glow, the past ignites,
A flicker of what used to be,
In the heart, our hope still fights,
For echoes hold eternity.

The Murmur of Starlight

In the stillness of the night,
Starlight whispers to the sky,
Each twinkle a tale of light,
That drifts on dreams that fly.

A gentle breeze carries the sound,
Of secrets shared among the stars,
In every shimmer, life is found,
Healing wounds, erasing scars.

Time flows like rivers through the dark,
Guiding hopes on silver streams,
Each star a flicker, each heart a spark,
Igniting the fabric of our dreams.

The cosmos hums a lullaby,
Soft and sweet, it wraps us near,
In its embrace, we learn to fly,
Expanding love, shedding fear.

For in the murmur of the night,
A universe awaits our gaze,
With starlit paths, a wondrous sight,
Leading us through endless maze.

The Softest Call

In twilight's whisper, shadows sway,
The softest call, a gentle play.
With every breath, the silence grows,
Where secrets bloom, no one knows.

Beneath the stars, a hush descends,
A world transformed, as daylight ends.
In dreams we wander, lost yet found,
In quiet moments, love's profound.

Through silver mist, we drift and glide,
In twilight's arms, we softly bide.
Each sigh a promise, sweet and clear,
In tender night, you draw me near.

With every heartbeat, time stands still,
In softest whispers, we feel the thrill.
A melody woven, soft and bright,
We'll chase the dawn, through endless night.

So hear the call, and take my hand,
In this soft space, together we stand.
With every note, our spirits soar,
In love's embrace, forevermore.

Gossamer Threads of Sound

Gossamer threads, they weave and twine,
In whispered tones, where dreams align.
A symphony of night, so clear,
Each note a dance, a voice we hear.

The breeze carries secrets, light as air,
In every rustle, a heartfelt prayer.
Melodic echoes from lands afar,
Each sound a story, a guiding star.

Crickets sing to the moonlit night,
A chorus born from sheer delight.
In every pulse, the world awakes,
As gossamer dreams in silence breaks.

With every heartbeat, whispers blend,
In harmonies that never end.
These fragile notes, like dreams unfurl,
In threads of sound, we weave our world.

So let us dance on air so light,
With gossamer songs that take their flight.
In fleeting moments, we find our place,
In woven sounds, we share our grace.

Secrets Linger in the Air

In twilight's haze, where shadows dwell,
Secrets linger, a quiet spell.
With every breath, a tale unfolds,
In whispered dreams, the heart beholds.

Among the trees, where secrets play,
The rustling leaves, they softly sway.
In every glance, a promise made,
In silent glances, love conveyed.

The stars above hold stories bright,
In cosmic dances, pure delight.
Each twinkle speaks of hopes and fears,
In whispered words, through fleeting years.

With gentle sighs, the night moves near,
As secrets linger, crystal clear.
In shadows deep, we find our way,
In hushed embraces, come what may.

So let us share what time bestows,
In tender moments, love only knows.
For in the air, where spirits soar,
Secrets linger, forevermore.

Unheard Songs of the Heart

In silence, listen, to the truth,
Unheard songs, of our lost youth.
A melody that sways, unseen,
Within the heart, where we have been.

Through echoing valleys, whispers flow,
In quiet chambers, feelings sow.
Each note a tear, each rise a dream,
In shadows cast, we drift and beam.

The pulse of love in every beat,
In melodies that softly greet.
Though words may falter, hearts attest,
In unheard songs, we find our rest.

So let the quiet reign supremely,
In every silence, hear it gleam.
For in the hush, the truth imparts,
The sweetest songs of our brave hearts.

Embrace the stillness, let it grow,
Unheard songs, in quiet glow.
In whispered tones, our spirits rise,
In love's embrace, we touch the skies.

The Unvoiced Symphony

In shadows deep, the silence plays,
A melody lost in dusky haze.
Notes unspoken fill the air,
Echoes linger everywhere.

Strings of heartbeats softly hum,
A rhythm found, yet never come.
Beauty wrapped in whispered sighs,
In the stillness, music lies.

Where dreams ascend on wings of sound,
In between the leaps, we're found.
The orchestra beyond our sight,
Plays through day and through the night.

Each moment holds a hidden tune,
Beneath the glow of silver moon.
A symphony that never ends,
In muted tones, our spirit bends.

So listen close, and you might find,
The unheard song that swells the mind.
In every breath, there lingers still,
An unvoiced symphony to thrill.

Secrets on the Wind

Gentle breezes carry tales,
Of hidden paths and whispered trails.
A hushed confession on the gust,
In every murmur, there is trust.

Leaves dance lightly, secrets spill,
Through cracked branches and low hills.
The winds weave stories rich and bright,
Painting the world in soft twilight.

In every rustle, truth is found,
Awakening dreams that dance around.
Silent wishes ride the tide,
Secrets on the wind, our guide.

With every breeze that graces skin,
Nature's voice calls us within.
It beckons softly to believe,
In every sigh, the heart's reprieve.

Listen close, enjoy the flight,
As secrets swirl in pure delight.
Through every gust, we learn to trust,
The whispers carried, kind and just.

The Intangible Melody

Floating softly, sounds unseen,
In the ether, serene and keen.
A tune that dances, light as air,
Transforms our thoughts, we pause and stare.

It spirals gently, a ghostly charm,
Wrapping shadows, keeping warm.
In silence lies a song of grace,
Echoes molded, time won't erase.

Notes linger near, just out of reach,
In a language only dreams can teach.
An invisible thread weaves profound,
The intangible melody we found.

With each heartbeat, it comes alive,
In the stillness, we learn to thrive.
A rhythm, soft as evening's glow,
The melody we yearn to know.

In twilight's arms, it starts to play,
A serenade that sweeps away.
In every breath, it finds its place,
The intangible melody we chase.

Whispers Between the Raindrops

When storms gather, a hush draws near,
Raindrops speak what we long to hear.
Softened voices blend and fall,
The sweetest whispers, nature's call.

Pattering rhythms, a gentle tune,
Echoing softly beneath the moon.
Each drop a secret, softly shared,
In every shower, hearts are bared.

Moving through shadows, they tell of grace,
Dancing freely, leaving no trace.
A chorus woven, interspersed,
In fleeting moments, we're immersed.

Embracing love in slickened streets,
Finding warmth where water meets.
In between the drops, we find,
New worlds waiting, intertwined.

So let the rain sing loud and clear,
Its wisdom whispers, drawing near.
Listen closely, trust the flow,
Whispers between the raindrops glow.

Whispers of the Endless Sky

Beneath the stars, dreams softly fade,
Silent wishes in twilight laid.
The moonlight dances on the crest,
As shadows find their quiet rest.

Clouds drift like whispers, ever so light,
Bearing secrets of the night.
A breeze carries tales from afar,
Filling hearts with a distant star.

Glimmers of hope in a vast expanse,
Weaving stories in a cosmic dance.
Each twinkle holds a promise true,
Beneath the endless sky, anew.

In twilight's embrace, dreams take flight,
Painting the heavens with soft insight.
The vastness whispers, never alone,
In the grand tapestry, we find our home.

Embers of night flicker and fade,
Guiding the lost in their serenade.
With every whisper from the sky,
Infinite wonders gently sigh.

The Soft Murmur of Nightfall

As daylight bows to evening's charm,
The world slows down, embraced, disarmed.
Crickets sing in a gentle tune,
While shadows stretch beneath the moon.

Trees rustle softly, secrets they keep,
As twilight settles, the earth's deep sleep.
Stars emerge, like whispers of light,
Painting the canvas of the night.

A soft murmur rolls through the air,
A lullaby only dreamers share.
In quiet corners, memories gleam,
As darkness cradles a fragile dream.

The night unfolds in velvety grace,
Wrapped in stillness, a sacred space.
With every sigh, the world holds tight,
To the soft murmur of the night.

A gentle breeze carries the tune,
Of hearts united under the moon.
With dreams unfurling in every beat,
Nightfall whispers, tranquil and sweet.

Sighs of the Wandering Heart

In the labyrinth of endless roam,
A heart searches for its long-lost home.
With every step, a silent plea,
For solace, where the soul is free.

Through forests thick and mountains high,
Wandering echoes beneath the sky.
Each sigh a story, old yet new,
In the tapestry of love's pursuit.

Rivers flow like thoughts unspoken,
Waves crash with whispers, hearts unbroken.
With every turn, the journey's art,
Is etched in sighs of the wandering heart.

Time slips softly, a fleeting friend,
In every moment, beginnings blend.
The road meanders, wild and vast,
Yet memories linger of the past.

In twilight's glow, beneath the stars,
The wandering heart knows no bars.
With open arms, it craves the light,
In every sigh, a spark ignites.

The Language of Lost Futures

In shadows cast by tomorrow's dreams,
   Lie whispers of what life redeems.
     Faded hopes in pages torn,
   Echoing futures yet to be born.

Time's gentle tide sweeps over the past,
   Carrying visions too bold, too vast.
     In the silence, a soft refrain,
The language of loss, a bittersweet gain.

With every heartbeat, a story unfolds,
   In the silence, a truth that beholds.
We weave our fate, thread by thread,
   In the spaces where angels tread.

Dreams drift like leaves on a stream,
Caught in the wake of a distant dream.
Yet in the whispers of what could be,
The language of lost futures sets us free.

   In every sigh, a choice is made,
   To honor the paths we often trade.
With open hearts, we embrace the night,
And speak the language of fading light.

The Breath of Quiet Dreams

In shadows soft where whispers play,
A world eludes, both night and day.
The gentle pulse of starlit skies,
Holds secrets deep, as silence sighs.

With every breath, a moment fades,
In twilight hush, the heart cascades.
Each note a thread of woven light,
A tapestry of velvet night.

The echoes swell, yet none can hear,
A lullaby that draws so near.
Like petals falling, grace unfolds,
In dreams, the truth of love retold.

Underneath the moon's embrace,
We dance in time, a slow-paced race.
The quiet dreams, a soft refrain,
Eclipsed by dawn, yet found again.

Embrace the still, the haunted gleam,
In every heart, the breath of dreams.
For though they wane, like fleeting light,
In silent depths, they'll take their flight.

Tender Tones in Twilight

As dusk descends with tender grace,
The world transforms, begins to trace.
A symphony of night unfolds,
In hues of purple, orange, golds.

The whispers of the fading sun,
Invite the night, its work begun.
With every star that dares to gleam,
Awakens softly, hopes and dreams.

Each note a caress, a sweet refrain,
In twilight's glow, we feel no pain.
The gentle flow of night's embrace,
Wraps every heart in softest lace.

With every breath, the daylight fades,
In hushed tones, the night cascades.
We linger here, where shadows sigh,
And softest dreams begin to fly.

Tender tones that fill the air,
Whispered secrets, free from care.
In twilight's arms, we find our rest,
And cherish moments we love best.

Linger of a Forgotten Lullaby

In corners where the shadows lie,
A soft refrain of days gone by.
The echoes of a tender song,
That lingers still, though time seems long.

Like whispers brushed on silent night,
The cradle's rock, a fleeting light.
Each note, a memory takes flight,
In dreams that dance beyond the sight.

The lullaby that once was sung,
In gentle tones, it softly clung.
To hearts that seek the warmth of soul,
The sweetest balm that makes us whole.

Yet as the shadows start to fade,
The songs we sing are never laid.
In every heart, they softly dwell,
The echo of a magic spell.

Remembered still, the nightingale,
In dreams, it whispers soft and pale.
A heartbeat wrapped in twilight's sigh,
The linger of a lullaby.

The Muffled Call of Distant Stars

In velvet skies where secrets hide,
The distant stars sing low, like tides.
A muffled call through cosmic streams,
That carries forth our deepest dreams.

Each twinkle holds a story spun,
Of ages past, when time was none.
Their whispered tunes, a mystic grace,
Guide wanderers through endless space.

We listen close, yet hear them far,
The hearts that yearn, the lost, the scarred.
In silent vows beneath their glow,
We find the paths we yearn to know.

Through midnight's veil, the charms align,
With wishes cast upon the line.
The muffled call, a guiding spark,
Awakens hope in shadows dark.

So linger here beneath the night,
Let stars ignite your inner light.
For in their songs, the world anew,
Awaits your heart, your dreams, your due.

The Soft Serenade of Shadows

In twilight's hush the shadows play,
They dance along the fading day.
Soft whispers weave through evening air,
As dreams take flight, shedding despair.

The moon's embrace, a silver sheen,
Cradles secrets, softly seen.
Beneath the stars, they softly sigh,
In silence, gently drifting by.

A lullaby, the darkness sings,
Of quiet hopes and tender things.
With every note, the night will rise,
And cradle us beneath the skies.

The chill of night, a tender touch,
Of fleeting moments, missed so much.
As shadows blend, they bid goodbye,
With every breath, a soft reply.

In shadows deep, the heart will weave,
A fabric rich, we must believe.
For in the dark, a light will gleam,
And guide us through, beyond the dream.

The Murmur of Time's Gentle Flow

Time drifts softly like a stream,
In its embrace, we find a dream.
Moments linger, then dissipate,
Leaving whispers, a gentle fate.

Through fields of gold, the hours fade,
Each heartbeat marks a serenade.
The ticking clock, a lullaby,
Tells tales of love and sorrow's sigh.

In every hour, the past remains,
Echoes softly in silent chains.
Endless cycles, the rise and fall,
Gently weaving through it all.

With every breath, the present gleams,
A fleeting dance of fragile dreams.
In the stillness, we learn to see,
The beauty in eternity.

So let the river take its course,
Embrace each moment, feel its force.
For in the flow, we learn to grow,
In time's embrace, our spirits glow.

Whispers of the Hidden Heart

Within the depths, the heart confides,
In whispered tones where love abides.
A secret garden, lush and wild,
Where hopes are born, and dreams beguiled.

Each thump a tale, a silent song,
Of journeys meant, where we belong.
The pulse of life, a steady beat,
In hidden chambers, bittersweet.

Veils of silence, softly drawn,
Reveal the light of breaking dawn.
In quiet corners, shadows blend,
With whispers meant to never end.

A treasure trove of memories bright,
That flicker softly in the night.
Each gentle sigh, a muse's call,
In twilight's arms, we rise, we fall.

So listen close, the heart will share,
Its fragile truths, laid open, bare.
A tender song, a fleeting glance,
In every breath, a hidden dance.

Hushed Tides of the Ancient Sea

The ocean's breath in tranquil curls,
Whispers ancient tales and swirls.
With every wave, a story weaves,
Of distant shores and autumn leaves.

Beneath the surface, secrets lie,
Of shipwrecked dreams and lullaby.
The tides, they ebb, the tides, they flow,
Carrying stories we long to know.

In salty air, the past unfolds,
Of sailors brave and treasures bold.
Each crashing wave sings history,
Hushed echoes of eternity.

The horizon calls with open arms,
A siren's song, a world of charms.
In the stillness, we find our way,
Guided by the moonlit spray.

So let us wander, hand in hand,
Along the shore, soft grains of sand.
For in the tides of time and sea,
We find the pulse of destiny.

Veiled Voices of the Heart

In shadowed corners whispers play,
Mysteries wrapped in soft decay.
A silent pull, a gentle sigh,
Lost tales beneath the evening sky.

Echoes linger, sweet yet rare,
Unseen forces pull the air.
Hidden dreams and silent calls,
Where truth resides behind the walls.

In secret chambers, feelings dwell,
A fondest wish we dare not tell.
Tender moments, soft and light,
Dance within the starry night.

Longing glances, fleeting grace,
The pulse of time, a warm embrace.
Softly spoken, hearts entwine,
Veiled in shadows, pure, divine.

Through whispered winds, we feel the start,
The language known to every heart.
These veiled voices, strong and sweet,
Guide us softly to our feet.

Gentle Hints in the Darkness

In twilight's grasp, the world slows down,
Soft whispers twirl, without a sound.
Hints of hope in shadows dwell,
A silent truth, a sacred spell.

Beneath the moon's soft silver glow,
Gentle breezes start to flow.
Each sigh a quaint, sweet refrain,
Glimmers of love in the rain.

Stars flicker softly overhead,
As dreams weave tales, carefully spread.
With every heartbeat, fears will fade,
In darkness, our courage is made.

Comfort wrapped in a tender night,
Navigating through fading light.
With gentle hints, we find our way,
In the shadows, we choose to stay.

Whispers linger, secrets twine,
Night's embrace, forever mine.
In hushed tones, life's truths are found,
Gentle hints that softly surround.

Soft Snatches of Lost Time

In faded pages, stories sleep,
Echoes of laughter, memories deep.
Soft snatches of what once was known,
In whispers of time, seeds are sown.

Through fleeting glances, moments hide,
In the fabric where dreams abide.
Threads of joy, and threads of pain,
Weaving tales in the soft rain.

Time glimmers like a distant star,
Each second counts, no matter how far.
In quiet corners, memories twine,
Unraveling softly, like aged wine.

With every heartbeat, shadows play,
Shifting colors of yesterday.
Soft snatches of lost time arise,
In the heart's deep, sacred skies.

Through golden glow of dusk's embrace,
We find the warmth of time's trace.
In gentle moments, life's sweet rhyme,
We cherish soft snatches of lost time.

Embraced by the Ethereal Breeze

In twilight's hue, the whispers soar,
Each breath a song, forevermore.
Embraced by winds that gently weave,
A tapestry of hearts that believe.

Softly dancing, leaves take flight,
Carrying dreams into the night.
With every gust, the world transforms,
Nature's grace, in silent forms.

With every sigh, the stars ignite,
Each moment filled with pure delight.
Wrapped in echoes of a soft tease,
We find ourselves in the ethereal breeze.

Through silvered paths where shadows sing,
Hope takes root, and courage springs.
In endless rhythm, life unwinds,
By the breeze, our hearts it finds.

In every touch, a promise stays,
The heart is swayed in tender ways.
Embraced by love, we softly seize,
The magic wrapped in the ethereal breeze.

Traces of Thoughts in the Ether

In the hush where silence meets,
Thoughts linger like fading beats.
Echoes dance in twilight's sway,
Time bends softly, slips away.

Fleeting moments weave the air,
Chasing shadows, light laid bare.
Wisps of dreams float near the ground,
In between, a truth is found.

Clouds drift slow with whispered grace,
In this soft, ethereal space.
Voices flicker, soft yet bright,
Painting colors into night.

Fragments of a distant past,
In the ether, shadows cast.
Thoughts unfurl like petals rare,
Breathing life into the air.

In every sigh, there's a thread,
Connected hearts where hope is fed.
In silence, life begins to bloom,
I find my peace amidst the gloom.

Reverberations of an Unearthly Calm

Underneath the endless dark,
Whispers stir, ignite a spark.
Stars hum softly, secrets shared,
In this stillness, hearts laid bare.

Moonlight drapes a silver sheet,
Cradles dreams, both light and fleet.
Echoes of the night unfold,
Stories waiting to be told.

The night air holds a gentle kiss,
Moments strung like beads of bliss.
Restless echoes, soft and low,
Guide the wandering souls below.

Chasing rhythms, soft and slow,
In the calm, we learn to grow.
Every heartbeat, a soft tune,
Dancing lightly 'neath the moon.

In reverie, we find our way,
As the dawn begins to play.
Unearthly peace, a silent balm,
Enwraps us in its tranquil calm.

The Quiet Drama of Dusk

When the sun begins to yield,
Day's bright laughter starts to shield.
Colors bleed in soft embrace,
Night unveils a quiet space.

Shadows stretch their gentle hands,
Painting hills and distant lands.
A symphony of hues sublime,
Notes of dusk in perfect time.

Nature holds her breath in peace,
Waiting for the dark's release.
Stars begin their quiet reign,
As whispers float like gentle rain.

The world sighs, in shades of gray,
Life's wild heart slows down to play.
In this moment, still and vast,
The drama blooms; shadows cast.

Embrace the calm, the soft descent,
In dusk's hold, we find content.
Stories linger on the breeze,
The quiet moment: purest ease.

Whispers from the Dreamweaver

In the realm where dreams take flight,
Softly woven threads of light.
The Dreamweaver softly hums,
Crafting tales as sleep becomes.

Fleeting visions beckon near,
Whispers softly in the ear.
Every sigh, a promise made,
In the twilight, dreams cascade.

Nestled in the arms of night,
Imaginations soar in flight.
Feathers brush, in softest glow,
Dancing freely, high and low.

Vistas bloom, the mind unfurls,
Painting wonders, hidden pearls.
Magic spun from silver strands,
Guiding us to distant lands.

In the dawn, the dreams will fade,
Yet the whispers still cascade.
In the heart, they hold a place,
The Dreamweaver's sweet embrace.

Silhouette of an Unheard Tune

In twilight's grasp, shadows dance,
Soft whispers weave through silent trance.
A melody lost in the gentle night,
Echoing dreams in fading light.

Hushed notes linger, sweetness in air,
Hints of a song, tender and rare.
Each flicker of stars sings a refrain,
Yet we remain wrapped in the mundane.

Ghostly rhythms brush past our ears,
Quiet but close, igniting our fears.
A sonnet drawn from the depths of our mind,
Elusive as time, yet lovingly kind.

In corners of thoughts where secrets lie,
We glimpse the harmony passing by.
A silhouette dances in dusk's embrace,
Yearning for someone to fill the space.

So we listen intently, hearts all aflame,
Hoping to capture the unheard name.
And though it may fade like a fleeting swoon,
We yearn still for that silhouette tune.

Murmurs on the Edge of Reality

In the depths where silence reigns,
Whispers entwine like ghostly chains.
Shadows flicker on the brink,
Where thoughts collide and memories sink.

Echoes of dreams, sharp and bright,
Skim the surface of day and night.
Fleeting glimpses of what could be,
A tapestry woven, yet hard to see.

In whispered tones, the truths collide,
Reality bends, nowhere to hide.
Each murmured word, a delicate thread,
Weaving the stories we'd rather not shed.

On edges defined by fear and grace,
We find ourselves in this sacred space.
Dancing shadows, drifting hopes,
Hold the weight of all our scopes.

Through veils of time, the secrets flow,
Murmurs of life, moving slow.
As the line between fades and frays,
We linger in dreams of endless days.

Inaudible Lullabies of the Universe

Beneath the stars, a soft refrain,
Cascading whispers, an endless chain.
Lullabies sung from worlds afar,
Wrapped in the light of a distant star.

Crickets chirp their nighttime song,
While shadows linger, lingering long.
The universe hums in tranquil tones,
Softly caressing our restless bones.

Each gentle breeze carries a plea,
Inaudible threads spun endlessly.
Dreams unfurl like petals at dawn,
In this vast expanse, we drift and yawn.

Time sways like the softest breeze,
Carving out space among the trees.
A lullaby cradles the weary heart,
In whispers of hope, we find our part.

So close your eyes, let the night unfold,
In the arms of the cosmos, mysteries told.
Inaudible songs wrap round like a shroud,
Embracing the quiet, profound yet loud.

The Softest Shades of Sound

In muted tones, colors collide,
A symphony played where echoes hide.
Brushstrokes of silence, gentle and sweet,
Wrap around hearts in rhythmic beat.

Whispers of past dance on the breeze,
Carrying secrets among the trees.
Tints of twilight, softening space,
A melody found in nature's grace.

Each note, a shadow, fleeting and light,
Paints a landscape where day turns to night.
In every heartbeat, a story unfolds,
Of feelings and moments that time gently holds.

The canvas of sound, a vibrant expanse,
Draws us closer, invites us to chance.
In the softest shades, we lose and we find,
Harmony waiting, eternally kind.

So listen closely, let silence resound,
In the softest shades, true beauty is found.
A serenade sung by the earth and the sky,
In the language of love, where dreams never die.

Whispering Woods Beneath the Moon

In the hush of night so deep,
The ancient trees sway and weep.
Moonlight dances on their leaves,
Secrets held in nature's eaves.

Crickets sing a lullaby,
As the stars adorn the sky.
Each shadow holds a mystery,
In the woods, where dreams run free.

Footsteps soft on mossy ground,
Whispers linger, all around.
The nightingale's sweet refrain,
Echoes softly through the glen.

Ferns unfurl and gently sway,
Guiding wanderers on their way.
The moonlight plays with every sound,
In this sacred, hallowed ground.

Breath of night, so calm and clear,
Fills the heart with soothing cheer.
In the woods, beneath the light,
The soul finds peace in endless night.

Faint Echoes of a Sigh

Whispers travel through the air,
Floating softly everywhere.
Faintest echoes, lost and found,
Resonate without a sound.

Time stands still, a fleeting pause,
In this moment, life's odd cause.
Breath concealed in silent sighs,
Carried softly, like the flies.

The clock ticks on, yet shadows stay,
Memories linger, fade away.
Gentle urges pull the heart,
In the silence, we depart.

Hopes and dreams like petals drift,
On the breeze, they give a gift.
In the quiet, truths reside,
Faint echoes of a sigh, confide.

Listen close to what's unsaid,
In the heart where thoughts are bred.
Faintest whispers tell the tale,
Of love that breathes, though it might pale.

Veils of Sound in the Morning Light

Morning breaks with soft delight,
Veils of sound greet the first light.
Chirping birds begin to sing,
A symphony of awakening.

Rustling leaves in gentle breeze,
Nature hums with perfect ease.
Footsteps on the dewy grass,
Moments cherished, fleeting, pass.

The dawn unfolds, a canvas bright,
Painting dreams in hues of light.
Echoes mingle, soft and sweet,
A new day's rhythm, calm and neat.

Streams of laughter, whispers blend,
In the light, all hearts can mend.
Every note a tender gift,
Carried on the breeze, they lift.

Life awakens with each sound,
In this symphony profound.
Veils of sound in morning's grace,
Find a home in nature's embrace.

The Secret Life of Silences

In the quiet, shadows dance,
Moments hang, a fleeting chance.
Silences hold stories deep,
Secrets that the heart must keep.

Every pause, a breath, a sigh,
Where unspoken words comply.
In stillness, truths begin to bloom,
Illuminating every room.

The hush of night, the calm of day,
Where thoughts and feelings gently sway.
Each silence like a whispered prayer,
A gentle hope, a tender care.

From the depths of quiet night,
Emerges strength, revealing light.
The rhythm beneath noise and cheer,
A secret life that draws us near.

Listen close, for there it lies,
In silent moments, wisdom sighs.
The secret life waits to be found,
In every hush, in every sound.

Silenced Beneath the Stars

In the night so deep and vast,
Whispers of dreams travel fast.
Stars blink low, a secret choir,
Filling the air with ancient fire.

Beneath the glow, shadows play,
Lost echoes drift, then fade away.
Night's embrace, a gentle sigh,
As silence weaves a lullaby.

The moon hangs low in velvet shrouds,
Cradling night's delicate clouds.
In this moment, hearts align,
Breath held tight, pure and divine.

Each twinkle tells a tale untold,
Of lovers' dreams and fables old.
In quietude, connections spark,
Guided softly through the dark.

As dawn approaches, light will swell,
But these whispered truths will dwell.
Beneath the stars, where silence reigns,
Our souls embrace, free of chains.

Hushed Voices in the Twilight

The day succumbs to twilight's grace,
Soft shadows dance in warm embrace.
A gentle hush, the world slows down,
As twilight weaves her golden gown.

Hidden whispers call the night,
Secrets shared, a soft delight.
In the fading light, hearts convene,
Finding solace in the serene.

Each star awakes as dusk draws near,
Murmurs of dreams they long to share.
In the calm, where hopes ignite,
Voices linger, glowing bright.

Time suspends, a fleeting spark,
In this dance, we leave a mark.
Together in a world of grey,
Our spirits soar, come what may.

A fleeting moment, a cherished bond,
In this twilight, we respond.
Hushed voices trace the evening's face,
In the twilight, we find our place.

The Language of Leaves

Rustling softly on the trees,
Each leaf tells tales with the breeze.
Whispers carried on the air,
Nature's poems, fleeting, rare.

In vibrant hues, the seasons speak,
Life's stories, both bold and meek.
Through storms and sun, they change their dress,
Each flutter holds a wilderness.

Gentle tones in sunlight's gleam,
Flickering shadows, nature's dream.
In every rustle, a secret found,
In emerald glades and golden ground.

When autumn comes with whispered sighs,
Leaves decay, yet never die.
They fall to earth, a graceful dance,
In every ending, a new chance.

The language of leaves forever flows,
In every color, in all that grows.
Through seasons' turn, their stories weave,
In every breath, you must believe.

Gentle Susurrus of Time

Time drips slowly, a soft refrain,
In whispered moments, joy and pain.
A gentle current, ever true,
Guiding hearts, stitching the new.

Past echoes linger, softly tread,
Memories dance, both tears and thread.
In fleeting glances, we find our way,
The sands of hours softly sway.

With each tick, the world unfolds,
Stories etched in moments bold.
Time hums softly, a calming song,
Inviting us to learn where we belong.

Days drift by, a shifting tide,
In time's embrace, we cannot hide.
Yet in each breath, renewal gleams,
A tapestry woven from our dreams.

So let us cherish the gentle flow,
In time's embrace, we learn to grow.
Each moment a treasure, softly spun,
In the susurrus, we are one.

Echoes in the Wind's Embrace

Whispers travel on the breeze,
Dancing leaves in gentle tease.
Stories carried, soft and clear,
Nature's song for all to hear.

Mountains echo with delight,
Cascades glimmer in the light.
Secrets held beneath the shade,
Fleeting moments never fade.

Stars awaken in the night,
Guiding dreams with silver light.
Every breeze a tender kiss,
In the air, a fleeting bliss.

Echoes linger, time stands still,
Calling forth each heart and will.
In the wind's embrace we find,
Harmony that knows no bind.

Listen close to every sigh,
Nature's voice will never die.
In the rustle, joy resounds,
Magic lives where peace abounds.

The Subtle Call of Distant Shores

Waves that lap on golden sands,
Echoes from the distant lands.
Salty air and whispered dreams,
Life unfolds in silver beams.

Footprints trace the paths of time,
Journeys woven in each rhyme.
Seagulls call with vibrant cheer,
Every moment crystal clear.

Sunrise paints the sky in hues,
Nature's palette, vibrant views.
Currents dance and stories flow,
Adventure waits where rivers go.

Hearts aligned with ocean's song,
In the tide, we all belong.
The horizon stretches wide,
Drawing souls to dream and glide.

In the twilight, shadows blend,
Chasing light as day must end.
The subtle call is ever near,
Whispers of what we hold dear.

Shadows that Sing at Midnight

In the silence, secrets hum,
Midnight's chorus, soft and numb.
Shadows dance with ethereal grace,
Every spirit finds its place.

Moonlight bathes the world in glow,
Where lost dreams and whispers flow.
Echoes of a past so dear,
Resonate for all to hear.

Stars align in cosmic play,
Guiding hearts that roam away.
Mysteries in dark unfold,
Stories waiting to be told.

In the stillness, magic brews,
Every note like morning dew.
Shadows weave their timeless song,
In the night, we all belong.

Bring your heart and leave your fears,
Let the shadows dry your tears.
In the midnight's gentle clasp,
Find the dreams that softly gasp.

Halos of Sound in the Twilight

As daylight fades and night awakes,
Twilight hums and softly shakes.
Halos form in soothing tones,
With every heartbeat, life condones.

Birds retreat to hidden nests,
Nature pauses, takes its rest.
Crickets start their evening song,
Aligning hearts that all belong.

Colors merge in soft embrace,
Moments linger, time and space.
Gentle whispers guide the way,
In this twilight where we stay.

Embers flicker, fireflies glow,
Bringing magic to the show.
Each note weaves a tapestry,
Of love, dreams, and harmony.

Close your eyes and breathe it in,
Let the music now begin.
As halos dance with every breath,
Find the beauty that won't rest.

The Whispering Veil of Night

In twilight's hush, the shadows creep,
The stars awake, their secrets deep.
A gentle breeze, a soft embrace,
The moonlight's touch, a silken grace.

Beneath the veil where dreams reside,
Whispers linger, hearts confide.
Each breath a tale, the night unfolds,
In silent realms, the magic molds.

A distant echo, a lover's sigh,
In the stillness, spirits fly.
The nightingale sings her sweet refrain,
Lost in the beauty of joy and pain.

Darkness wraps in tender shrouds,
Glimmers dance amidst the clouds.
A tapestry of secrets spun,
The night is ours, till day be done.

With every star, a wish is cast,
In the whispering night, shadows last.
Time drifts slowly, each moment pure,
In night's embrace, we find the cure.

Echoes in the Hourglass

Time slips softly through our hands,
Like grains of sand on distant strands.
Each moment fleeting, whispers lost,
In echoes past, we count the cost.

The hourglass holds our dreams and fears,
Each tick a canvas of silent tears.
We chase the seconds, quick and fleet,
Yet wisdom lies in moments sweet.

A heartbeat echoes, faint yet clear,
In the chambers of our quiet sphere.
We gather shadows, we weave the light,
In the silent dance of day and night.

Memories linger, like faded paint,
On walls of time, where hopes don't faint.
The hourglass whispers, tales unfold,
Of paths we walked, both meek and bold.

In grains of time, our stories merge,
Each echo fuels a silent surge.
We'll find our strength, as moments flee,
In echoes of what was meant to be.

Ripples of Unseen Sorrows

Beneath the surface, waters churn,
Unseen sorrows in silence burn.
A gentle wave, a quiet ache,
In hidden depths, our hearts will break.

The stillness hides what pain can't show,
In tranquil guise, emotions flow.
Each ripple speaks a secret tale,
Of lives entwined, where shadows sail.

A breath of sorrow, whispered low,
In the depths where few will go.
Through fractured mirrors, reflections blend,
In quiet moments, we pretend.

Yet through the pain, the light breaks through,
As dawn arrives, with colors new.
The ripples fade, but scars remain,
In whispered echoes, love and pain.

In every heart, a story's found,
Of unseen sorrows, tightly wound.
But through the dark, hope gently gleams,
In ripples soft, we find our dreams.

Silken Threads of Silence

In the stillness, woven tight,
Silken threads embrace the night.
Each whisper soft, each breath a sigh,
In silence deep, our spirits fly.

Glistening seams of fragile grace,
In quiet corners, we find our place.
A tapestry of thoughts unfurled,
In woven silence, a hidden world.

The fabric hums, a gentle tune,
Beneath the glow of silver moon.
Knotted dreams in hidden seams,
In silence laced with whispered themes.

As shadows dance and stars align,
In silken threads, our hearts entwine.
Each moment stitched in love's embrace,
In quietude, we find our grace.

Through silken threads, connections bind,
The heart's own rhythm, soft and kind.
In silent spaces, truths are found,
In threads of silence, we are bound.

Echoes That Dissent from Darkness

In the shadow, whispers weave,
Soft voices rise, though few believe.
They challenge night with resolute light,
Each echo sparks the heart's insight.

Flickering flames dance in the void,
Resilient souls, never destroyed.
They find their strength in unity's call,
Together they stand, they shall not fall.

Beneath the weight of silence lies,
The truth that time can never disguise.
With courage bold, they face the fray,
And turn the night to brightening day.

In every corner, laughter stirs,
As hope ignites, despair demurs.
The echoes swell, a vibrant tune,
Defying gloom beneath the moon.

So let the dark no longer reign,
In hearts awakened, love will gain.
For echoes that dissent from fear,
Shall pave the path for all who steer.

Stories Carried by the Wind

Whispers flutter through the trees,
Tales of life shared on the breeze.
From ancient times to present day,
Each story finds its unique way.

Mountains echo with forgotten lore,
Of dreams and hopes that once did soar.
The wind spins yarns of joy and woe,
Painting the world with highs and low.

From distant lands, the voices blend,
Creating paths that twist and bend.
Carried forth on gentle sighs,
New tales emerge beneath the skies.

Beneath the stars, the night unfolds,
Revelations in each breath retold.
Interwoven like threads of fate,
These tales unite, they never wait.

So listen close for nature's lore,
The wind is rich with stories more.
For every breeze that gently sings,
Holds the magic of living things.

The Pulse of Silent Shadows

In the stillness, secrets dwell,
Silent shadows weave their spell.
A heartbeat felt within the night,
Whispers dance just out of sight.

Softly echoing through the air,
The world breathes deep, a quiet prayer.
Each pulse carries a tale untold,
In shadow's grasp, the brave and bold.

They wander paths of muted grace,
Embracing time in every space.
With every beat, new dreams awake,
In shadows' arms, hearts gently break.

Hidden truths in silence bloom,
Filling voids with soft perfume.
The pulse of life in shadows hums,
As night enfolds, the future comes.

So hear the depth of whispered beats,
In every heart, the darkness greets.
For in the pulse of silent night,
Love lingers long, a guiding light.

The Hidden Song of Serenity

In gentle waves that kiss the shore,
A hidden song forevermore.
Each note, a breath steeped in calm,
A quiet balm, a soothing psalm.

Beneath the surface, life takes flight,
A melody unseen, pure delight.
Harmony weaves through every frame,
In softest whispers, love proclaims.

The rustling leaves, the flowing stream,
Nature's sound invites a dream.
From dawn's first light to twilight's hue,
Serenity sings forever true.

In stillness found in-depth of night,
Moments cherished, hearts ignite.
The hidden song calls each to share,
The beauty found in moments rare.

So let the world around us pause,
In silent gaze, we find the cause.
The hidden song of peace resounds,
Uniting souls where love abounds.

Secrets Carried on a Distant Wind

Whispers float on gentle breeze,
Tales of dreams and silent pleas.
Hidden paths by moonlight kissed,
Echoes of the night persist.

Stars align, the skies conspire,
Hearts entwined like wisps of fire.
Carried far, their stories blend,
In the arms of night, they tend.

Listen close, the secrets bare,
Rustling leaves, a subtle air.
In the hush, the world reveals,
What the heart most truly feels.

Journey forth, the dawn will break,
Trust the dreams that you will make.
For in whispers, truth is spun,
The tale continues, never done.

Murmurs of the Forgotten Forest

Underneath the ancient boughs,
Nature hums eternal vows.
Footsteps fade on mossy ground,
In this realm, lost voices sound.

Ferns unfurl with tender grace,
Shadows dance in secret space.
Each moment holds a story old,
A tapestry of green and gold.

Windswept sighs through tangled trees,
Carry echoes, whispers tease.
Memory weaves through roots and stone,
In the forest, we're not alone.

Let the whispers guide your way,
To forgotten dreams that sway.
In the heart where shadows lie,
Listen close and you'll hear why.

Whispers of the Hidden Depths

In the silence of the deep,
Secrets dwell that time will keep.
Rippling waters, shadows gleam,
Lost in depths, we dare to dream.

Dive beneath the surface cool,
Find the treasures, ancient rule.
Every drop a story spun,
Every current softly run.

Voices calling from the dark,
Hidden truths that leave a mark.
In the silence, still they wait,
Guardians of a whispered fate.

So we plunge, and so we hear,
What lies buried, faint yet clear.
In the depths, our hearts will find,
The whispers sweet, forever kind.

Ephemeral Sounds of the Soul

Fleeting notes, a hush of grace,
Voices dance in empty space.
Moments cling like autumn leaves,
In their beauty, the heart believes.

Echoes fade in twilight's glow,
Gentle ripples ebb and flow.
Chasing whispers, soft and bright,
Soulful songs declare the night.

In every breath, a story flows,
As the timeless river grows.
Listen close, the world will sing,
To the heart, the joy they bring.

Melodies of fleeting hours,
Fill the air with magic powers.
In this space, our spirits soar,
Ephemeral, yet wanting more.

Conversations with the Unknown

In shadows soft, we dare to tread,
Where whispers drift, and words go dead.
Mysteries murmur in the hush of night,
Echoes dance just out of sight.

Thoughts like leaves, they spin and sway,
Carried by winds that twist and play.
We ask the stars for tales untold,
Secrets wrapped in silver and gold.

Questions linger on the breath we share,
In the silence, we find a rare flair.
A fleeting glance, a moment's grace,
In the unknown, we find our place.

Beyond the veil, what lies ahead?
Paths unseen, where few have tread.
Each whisper holds a spark of light,
Guiding our way through the endless night.

To converse with shadows, a dance of thought,
In realms untouched, where time is caught.
With every heartbeat, we resonate,
In conversations with the unknown fate.

Hidden Cadences of the Night

When darkness falls, a tune is played,
In quiet corners, dreams cascade.
The moonbeams weave a delicate thread,
Soft melodies where thoughts are fed.

Crickets chirp their evening song,
Where hidden rhythms stir along.
A tapestry of whispers, sweet and low,
In the night's embrace, our spirits grow.

Rustling leaves sigh softly in time,
Nature's pulse, alive and prime.
Each heartbeat echoes in the dark,
Filling the silence with a spark.

In the cool breeze, echoes entwine,
Carrying secrets, both yours and mine.
The universe hums a gentle tune,
In the cradle of night under the moon.

Let us dance to the rhythms we find,
In the vastness, our souls aligned.
With hidden cadences that softly play,
We'll lose ourselves in night's ballet.

The Barest Hints of Emotion

In silent glances, feelings bloom,
Soft as shadows in a dim-lit room.
Unspoken words float gently near,
The barest hints, they draw us near.

A touch, a sigh, a fleeting glance,
In the quiet, our hearts advance.
Whispers tangled in the air,
Hints of longing, a silent prayer.

Each heartbeat shared, a tender thread,
Carving paths where words dare not tread.
Moments stitched with fragile care,
In the silence, emotions dare.

The lightest brush of fingertips,
Tells of tales that linger on lips.
Beneath the stars, our souls collide,
In the barest hints, where love can't hide.

So let us linger in this place,
Amid the whispers, the soft embrace.
For in these hints, we find a home,
In the silence, love's seeds are sown.

Whispering Roots Beneath the Earth

Beneath the ground, roots intertwine,
In secret chambers, they align.
Whispering tales of storms and sun,
A dance of life that's just begun.

Hidden pathways weave and wind,
In the dark, connections find.
Life's quiet murmurs sing their song,
In the depths where we all belong.

With every stretch, they seek and grasp,
Embracing earth in tender clasp.
In the hush, a story unfolds,
Of ancient whispers and dreams retold.

The pulse of life runs deep within,
In the shadows, we lose and win.
A tapestry woven, silent, profound,
Whispering roots in the sacred ground.

Through storms and seasons, they remain,
A testament to joy and pain.
Each breath they take, a bond we share,
In the quiet earth, we find our care.

Resonating Memories in the Quiet

In shadows deep, where silence stirs,
Faded echoes of laughter gently purrs.
Each whisper held in twilight's grasp,
A tender touch, a gentle clasp.

Through closed eyes, the past resides,
In silent corners, where deep joy hides.
Memories dance on a fragile breeze,
Rustling leaves in the ancient trees.

Softly spoken, the tales unwind,
Of love once lost, but never blind.
Each moment cherished, like a song,
Resonating with voices long.

The heart remembers, through dusk and dawn,
As light fades softly, anew it's drawn.
In quiet corners of the soul,
Resonating memories fill the whole.

Distant Echoes of the Past

Hushed winds carry a whispering song,
Of days gone by, where we belong.
Fleeting glimpses through time's open door,
Echoes of laughter, of love, and more.

In twilight's glow, shadows play,
Telling tales of yesterday.
A heartbeat echoes, a teardrop's fall,
The past is alive, in each rise and call.

Moments shimmer like stars on the bay,
Fleeting glimpses of a brighter day.
In every sigh, a memory caught,
Distant echoes, never forgot.

Whispers linger, soft and sweet,
Tracing paths where hearts would meet.
Through tangled threads of fate's design,
The distant past still intertwines.

The Language of Unspoken Thoughts

In silence speaks the heart's own song,
Words unsaid, where feelings belong.
Each glance exchanged holds a story,
A secret language, veiled in glory.

Through uncharted realms of souls entwined,
The echo of love gently aligned.
In simple gestures, deep worlds form,
Unspoken thoughts, a quiet storm.

In every pause, in every sigh,
The language flows, never shy.
In heartbeats shared, a bond we forge,
Through silent realms, our spirits merge.

Words may falter, and voices fade,
Yet in the silence, truth is laid.
Unspoken thoughts, a sacred art,
Whispered softly, heart to heart.

Whispers of the Wandering Stars

Underneath a blanket of night,
Stars sing softly, pure delight.
In cosmic trails, their secrets spin,
Whispers of dreams, where journeys begin.

Each twinkling light, a tale to share,
Of hopes and wishes tossed in the air.
The universe breathes a gentle sigh,
While celestial bodies dance and fly.

Through endless skies, we drift and roam,
Finding solace, in the stars' wide dome.
In quiet nights, our spirits soar,
Whispers linger, forever more.

In twilight's embrace, the cosmos gleams,
Dreams intertwine with the starlit beams.
With every pulse of the night sky bright,
Whispers of stars guide us with light.

Echoes in the Breeze

Softly the leaves begin to sway,
Crickets sing as night meets day.
Whispers carried on the air,
Memories linger, everywhere.

Stars above begin to peek,
Nature hums, a gentle speak.
Footsteps lost in whispered sound,
In the stillness, peace is found.

Cool winds dance through branches high,
Tales of yesterdays drift by.
Echoes fade but never cease,
In this moment, find your peace.

Hushed the world in twilight's glow,
Where dreams and hopes begin to flow.
Each sigh a story, each breath a song,
In this night, we all belong.

Beneath the sky, hearts intertwine,
In the silence, souls align.
Listen close, the breezes tease,
Carrying life's sweet melodies.

Secrets of the Quiet Night

Underneath the silver moon,
Shadows dance and softly croon.
Stars conceal their precious light,
Guarding secrets of the night.

In the stillness, whispers bloom,
Softly sweeping through the gloom.
Every heartbeat echoes low,
In the dark, we come to know.

Voices linger, faint and near,
Caught between hope and fear.
In the silence, truth unveils,
Like gentle winds that fill the sails.

Time stands still, a fleeting chance,
In the night, a secret dance.
Every sigh, a story told,
In the dark, our dreams unfold.

Close your eyes, let silence speak,
In the night, it's peace we seek.
Secrets hidden, softly bright,
Unravel in the quiet night.

Murmurs in Shadowed Corners

In the shadows, secrets lie,
Woven tales of days gone by.
Murmurs echo soft and clear,
Whispered thoughts for those who hear.

Cornered dreams take flight in light,
Glimmers fading into night.
Silent hopes in corners stay,
Waiting for the break of day.

Invisible threads softly entwine,
Lost in thoughts like fragile wine.
Each murmur holds a world apart,
A tapestry of every heart.

Gently woven, tales unfurl,
In the shadows, thoughts can twirl.
Listen closely, feel the beat,
In the quiet, life's discreet.

Through the dark, whispers flow,
Murmurs tell us what to know.
In the corners, truths abide,
Hidden deep where dreams collide.

Whispers of Forgotten Dreams

Drifting softly through the haze,
Whispers of long-lost days.
Every dream a fleeting sigh,
Echoes drifting, floating by.

Voices fading like the mist,
Past and present coexist.
In the night, a silent call,
Memories rise, we hear them all.

Glimmers of what once could be,
In our hearts, they wander free.
Forgotten hopes on softest wings,
Back to life, the spirit sings.

Hold them close, don't let them fade,
In our hearts, the dreams we made.
Whispers echo, softly gleam,
Illuminating every dream.

Through the shadows, light will creep,
Awakening the dreams we keep.
In the night, they softly gleam,
Whispers of forgotten dream.

Breezes Carrying Memories

Gentle winds through the trees,
Whisper tales of long ago,
Carried high on summer's breath,
Where laughter's echoes softly flow.

Old photographs in the air,
Moments lost but not erased,
Every gust a fleeting thought,
In memory's sweet embrace.

Days of sunshine, dreams so bright,
Fleeting moments, yet they last,
Breezes dance with past delights,
A symphony, the shadows cast.

In the twilight, secrets sigh,
Beneath the stars, the stories swell,
Nature's lullaby nearby,
Every breeze a whispered spell.

So let the winds carry me,
Through the corridors of time,
In the heart, memories gleam,
Like old poems in their rhyme.

Shadows That Hold My Name

In the dusk, shadows stretch wide,
Woven threads of moonlit grace,
They dance softly, side by side,
Carrying whispers of my place.

Each silhouette, a ghostly friend,
Echoes of my past remain,
In their arms, it feels like home,
Shadows that hold my name.

Silent watchers of my dreams,
Guardians of the night unfurled,
In their depths, the lost light gleams,
A canvas of my hidden world.

When the night begins to fade,
And the dawn wraps its embrace,
Shadows linger, softly laid,
An intimate and tender space.

They will follow where I roam,
In the light and in the dark,
Carrying whispers of my soul,
Shadows that leave their mark.

Subdued Echoes of the Past

Softly hums the ancient trees,
With whispers from a time long gone,
In their rustle, secrets freeze,
Echoes linger with the dawn.

Footsteps fade on forgotten paths,
Memories drift like fallen leaves,
In their stillness, time that laughs,
Telling tales that the heart weaves.

In the silence, ghosts abide,
Faces seen in shadows thin,
Every sigh a step aside,
Remembered warmth held deep within.

Through the years, the echoes call,
Rekindling warmth in fleeting light,
In quiet moments, I recall,
Subdued echoes of the night.

Past and present intertwine,
In the whispers of the breeze,
Every note a soft design,
A song that time will never cease.

The Quiet Heartbeat of Nature

In the hush of morning light,
Nature breathes a gentle sigh,
Each heartbeat, a pure delight,
A soft pulse as moments fly.

Leaves flutter like whispered dreams,
In the stillness, creatures stir,
The rhythm flows with silent streams,
Nature's song, a quiet purr.

Mountains stand in stoic grace,
Guardians of the timeworn days,
In their shadows, a sacred space,
A sacred tune that softly plays.

Clouds drift high, a painter's hand,
Crafting tales in skies so blue,
With every swirl, a quiet plan,
Nature speaks in shades of hue.

So listen close, the heart beats here,
In every rustle, every sound,
In nature's arms, there's nothing to fear,
A quiet pulse that knows no bound.

Soft Shadows Speak

In twilight's gentle hush, they sigh,
Whispers of the night drift by.
Silhouettes dance in muted light,
Echoes of secrets take flight.

Moonbeams weave through leaf and tree,
Curtains of dusk, soft as can be.
Each flicker a tale of yore,
Moments that linger, forevermore.

Shadows linger, holding grace,
Hidden truths in every space.
Through silence, they softly share,
Stories we live, yet seldom dare.

In the corners where dreams convene,
Soft shadows paint a world unseen.
Fragrant night air fills the vale,
Life's hidden magic in every tale.

So listen close as shadows play,
Their whispers will guide our stray.
In their folds, find calm delight,
Soft shadows speak in the night.

A Breath of Subtle Darkness

In realms where daylight speaks farewell,
A breath of dusk begins to swell.
Shadows stretch and softly swell,
Wrapping the earth in their mellow spell.

Stars awaken one by one,
A dance of night just has begun.
The cool breeze carries tales long spun,
In the hush, our thoughts are won.

Mysterious paths beckon forth,
Dancing shadows of hidden worth.
With every step, the heart uncovers,
The beauty found in darkened covers.

Silence speaks the loudest here,
In subtle darkness, all is clear.
Listen to the secrets near,
A breath of night holds what we fear.

Enveloped in this velvet dome,
In shadows, we find peace and home.
Each sigh of night is woven tight,
A breath of subtle darkness, pure light.

The Unseen Serenade

Listen close to the silent song,
Echoes of night, where hearts belong.
A serenade without a sound,
In stillness, our dreams abound.

Stars hum softly in cosmic light,
Guiding souls through the velvet night.
A melody that weaves the air,
Notes of longing, free from care.

In shadows, the music finds its way,
Breaking the dawn, keeping night at bay.
With every echo, memories weave,
The unseen serenade, we believe.

Feel the rhythm pulse within,
A gentle tug, where dreams begin.
In whispered tones, hope is laid,
In night's embrace, we are not afraid.

Through the dark, let your spirit soar,
In the unseen, there's so much more.
Harmony flows from heart to heart,
The unseen serenade, a work of art.

Veiled Sounds of Solitude

In the stillness, a heartbeat thrums,
Veiled sounds of solitude softly hums.
Each sigh of silence cleaves the air,
In whispered breaths, we truly dare.

Gentle echoes find their place,
Shadows dance with a tender grace.
The world outside begins to fade,
In solitude, dreams are laid.

Rustling leaves and distant calls,
Each sound a treasure, each silence enthralls.
In the quiet, thoughts intertwine,
Veiled sounds of solitude, divine.

Moments whisper secrets deep,
Inviting us into quiet sleep.
In solitude's arms, we mend our souls,
Listening close as the night unfolds.

So linger long in the midnight's hold,
In veiled sounds, let your heart be bold.
Within the stillness, we may find,
The music of solitude, entwined.

Secrets Beneath the Stillness

In the quiet grove, whispers weave,
Leaves unfold tales that hearts believe.
Beneath the moon's soft, tender light,
Secrets linger in the still of night.

Silent streams hum their ancient song,
Ripples echo where shadows belong.
Roots of the trees hold stories untold,
In every grain, a memory bold.

The stars blink gently, a knowing gaze,
Hidden wonders in twilight's haze.
Eyes close softly, dreams take their flight,
In the hush, find solace, in the night.

The air bears scents of pine and earth,
Each breath a promise, a whispered birth.
Time stands still as darkness unfolds,
Secrets beneath the silence, stories of old.

When dawn awakens with golden rays,
The secrets fade in the morning's gaze.
Yet in the stillness, they softly dwell,
Waiting for hearts that feel them well.

Shadows Speak Softly

In the fading light, shadows play,
Dancing gently at the end of day.
With whispers low and voices sweet,
They tell of moments lost, bittersweet.

Beneath the trees where silence grows,
Echoes of laughter in breezes blows.
Mysteries wrapped in twilight's veil,
Listen closely to the stories they tell.

The nightingale sings a soft refrain,
Memories drift like the softest rain.
In every corner where darkness lies,
Shadows speak softly, wisdom from the skies.

Dreams intertwine with the closing light,
In the tender arms of encroaching night.
Each shadow holds a piece of the past,
Speaking gently, their messages vast.

As stars awaken, their glow ignites,
The shadows dance with the cool of nights.
In hushed tones, they share with grace,
The beauty found in a quiet space.

Subtle Sounds of Serenity

Whispers of leaves in a gentle breeze,
Carry the notes of tranquil ease.
Water flows softly over smooth stone,
In nature's cradle, we're never alone.

The call of a bird, a soft cooing sigh,
Brings peace to the heart, as moments fly.
Clouds drift by in a silent parade,
In subtle sounds, a calm serenade.

Moonlight glimmers on the water's face,
A tender embrace of nature's grace.
Each breath is a gift, a moment to cherish,
In the symphony soft, all worries perish.

The rustle of grass, the flutter of moths,
Nature's orchestra, gentle and soft.
Each sound a reminder of life's sweet song,
In subtle tones, we all belong.

As daylight fades into evening's fold,
Healing tones wrap us in warmth untold.
In every note, find solace and glee,
In subtle sounds, discover the key.

Hushed Conversations of Dusk

When the sky blushes in twilight hue,
Hushed conversations begin anew.
Whispers linger in the fading light,
As day gives way to the embrace of night.

The horizon blushes, a velvet spread,
Stories forgotten, now gently tread.
With each gentle breeze, tales are spun,
In dusk's soft grasp, a day is done.

Stars begin twinkling, a celestial choir,
Echoing secrets of heart and desire.
In gatherings quiet, we share, we sigh,
Hushed conversations as time slips by.

The moon takes its throne, a tranquil guide,
Illuminating paths where shadows reside.
In the stillness, quiet minds converse,
The beauty of dusk, an unspoken verse.

In this gentle space, our spirits soar,
Finding connection in the evermore.
As day departs, and night draws near,
Hushed conversations, a voice we hear.

Eloquent Murmurs of Memory

In shadows deep, whispers arise,
Echoes of laughter, silenced cries.
Time drapes softly, a tender shroud,
Moments linger, lost in a crowd.

Faded photographs, corners worn,
Memories bloom, though they are torn.
Slides of faces, a wistful kiss,
Captured in twilight, a fleeting bliss.

With every heartbeat, stories unfold,
In the silence, secrets retold.
Ghosts of the past weave through the night,
Eloquent murmurs, fading from sight.

A flicker of light on dusty shelves,
Reminders of dreams once lived by selves.
Quiet reflections in a moonlit stream,
Holding the fabric of each lost dream.

As silence deepens, shadows entwine,
In the echoes of time, we still shine.
Whispers of memory, tender and bright,
A dance of the past bathed in soft light.

Shy Songs of Forgotten Meadows

In meadows where wildflowers bloom,
Soft melodies chase away the gloom.
Breezes carry whispers, so sweet,
Nature sings softly, beneath our feet.

Shadows of trees, a gentle sway,
Dancing to songs that drift away.
Butterflies flit, a fleeting refrain,
Bright colors merge with the gentle rain.

The sun dips low, painting the skies,
As twilight hums, the day slowly dies.
Crickets awaken, their voices soft,
With shy songs rising, they lift us aloft.

Stars sprinkle light on this tranquil sea,
Where dreams unfold, and spirits are free.
In each rustle, in every breeze,
The shy songs echo through willow trees.

Time flows gently, like a river's grace,
Unfolding stories in a sacred space.
And as we linger, hearts open wide,
Shy songs of meadows become our guide.

The Delicate Fabric of Sound

In threads of silence, vibrations weave,
The delicate fabric, what we believe.
Notes rise and fall, like waves on the shore,
Whispers entwined, forevermore.

Strings plucked gently, a heartfelt plea,
Melodies dance, setting spirits free.
Harmony echoes in twilight's embrace,
Emotions reflected in every space.

Rhythms cascade, like rain from above,
Breath of the earth, the pulse of love.
Sonorous whispers in twilight's glow,
The symphony of life, a gentle flow.

With every heartbeat, music unfurls,
A tapestry woven with laughter and swirls.
In the stillness, in the quiet hours,
The delicate fabric opens its flowers.

Each note a story, a path to explore,
Binding us close, forever and more.
In the orchestra of life, we belong,
The delicate fabric sings its song.

Ghostly Chords in the Autumn Breeze

Through rustling leaves, whispers arise,
Ghostly chords under the dusky skies.
Echoes of laughter from days gone by,
The autumn breeze sings a haunting sigh.

Bare branches sway in the chilly air,
Carrying secrets, memories rare.
Shadows grow long, as daylight wanes,
Ghostly harmonies weave through the lanes.

Crimson and gold adorn the ground,
In this vast silence, ghosts are found.
Each fluttering leaf tells a tale far and wide,
Ghostly chords in the breeze, our hearts confide.

As twilight descends, the world softly hums,
Reminders of echoes from time's gentle drums.
In the whispering night, we pause and reflect,
Ghostly chords linger, a timeless connect.

In the midst of this chill, warmth is still near,
Through the autumn air, love's song we hear.
In the twilight's embrace, together we stand,
Ghostly chords in the breeze, forever hand in hand.

Quiet Tales Beneath the Canopy.

In the woods where shadows play,
Branches sway and gently sway,
Softly spoken, nature's grace,
Tales unfold in quiet space.

Whispers of the leaves above,
Dancing lightly, full of love,
Every rustle tells a tale,
In the breath of wind, we sail.

Moonlight filters through the green,
Casting dreams we've rarely seen,
Footsteps echo on the floor,
Of the earth, where spirits soar.

Crickets sing their evening tune,
Stars awaken, one by one,
Night's embrace, a soothing balm,
Resting hearts, so safe and calm.

Beneath the canopy so bright,
Life unfurls in shared delight,
In the stillness, hope prevails,
As we weave our quiet tales.

Echoes of the Silent Night

Underneath a velvet sky,
Stars like diamonds, oh so high,
In the hush, the world does sleep,
Echoes of the night are deep.

Moonlit paths where shadows dance,
Lost in whispers, lost in trance,
Gentle breezes softly sigh,
Bringing secrets from the sky.

Rippling waters, glistening bright,
Mirror dreams in silver light,
Every echo softly calls,
In the night, where magic falls.

Stillness wraps the world in peace,
Time stands still; our thoughts release,
In the shadows, truth takes flight,
Finding solace in the night.

As we wander, hearts in tune,
Feeling echoes of the moon,
In the silence, hope ignites,
Whispers thread through starry nights.

Whispers in the Gloaming

At the edge of day's retreat,
Colors blend and softly meet,
In the gloaming, light will fade,
Nature's whispers, dreams are made.

Softly as the night unfurls,
Magic swirls in shadows, twirls,
Murmured secrets, soft and low,
In the twilight, stories flow.

Gentle breezes breathe and sigh,
Light a candle, don't be shy,
In the fading warmth's embrace,
Feel the whispers, find your place.

As the stars begin to gleam,
Close your eyes and dream a dream,
In this twilight, softly roam,
Whispers guide you safely home.

In the hush, the heart takes wing,
Footsteps light, as night birds sing,
Underneath the purple dome,
In the gloaming, we find home.

Murmurs of the Moonlit Path

On the trail where moonbeams glow,
Silver light like rivers flow,
Every step a whispered sound,
In the night, our hearts are found.

Leaves rustle with secrets old,
Tales of love and dreams retold,
As we walk, the shadows play,
Guiding us along the way.

Crickets serenade the stars,
Nature's hymn, no need for bars,
In the stillness, fears depart,
Join the murmurs of the heart.

Beneath the sky, the world is wide,
In the moonlight, fears subside,
Hand in hand, we journey forth,
Finding joy, embracing worth.

As the night calls out our name,
Every moment feels the same,
In the moonlit path we tread,
Murmurs whisper, gently spread.

An Echo of Forgotten Lullabies

In the stillness of night, whispers fade,
Songs of old, in shadows played.
Memory cradles each gentle tone,
Lost in the fog, we drift alone.

Stars above weave tales untold,
Echoes of dreams, both faint and bold.
Crickets sing their nightly refrain,
In the silence, there's sweet pain.

Lullabies linger, soft and low,
Carried by winds that ebb and flow.
Hearts remember each tender phrase,
In the night's hush, we find our ways.

Moonlight dances on the ground,
In its glow, lost hopes are found.
Each sigh we share, a timeless grace,
Finding our solace, face to face.

These echoes haunt like shadows cast,
Reminders of futures that came to pass.
Yet in the twilight, joy takes flight,
An echo of love in the quiet night.

Reverberations of a Fading Day

As the sun dips low, colors blend,
In twilight's grasp, where shadows mend.
Whispers linger on the breeze,
Time slows down, a gentle tease.

Golden hues paint the sky bright,
Fading softly into night.
Each moment stretches, pure and rare,
As silence wraps us in its care.

Footsteps echo through the dusk,
In this hour, we find our trust.
Nature sighs, a soft retreat,
Day's reverberations feel complete.

Stars emerge in twinkling grace,
Each a memory, a glowing trace.
In the dark, dreams start to play,
A symphony of hopes on display.

The day departs, yet dreams remain,
A canvas stretched by joy and pain.
In the shadows, new paths wend,
To dusk we yield, with hearts to mend.

Ethereal Musings in Dusk

When day meets night, a hush unfolds,
Mysteries whispered, gently told.
In the dusk, where light meets shade,
The heart's secrets are softly laid.

Chasing whispers on the breeze,
Moments linger with gentle ease.
Beneath the veil of fading light,
Thoughts take flight, hearts feel the height.

Colors bleed, a painter's stroke,
In this quiet, the soul awoke.
Ethereal dances twist and swirl,
In twilight's arms, we dream and twirl.

Reflections shimmer in the air,
An ethereal grace of what we share.
Fleeting visions, soft and slight,
In dusk's embrace, we find our light.

Each thought a thread in the tapestry,
Woven together, a shared decree.
In the stillness, we find our way,
Ethereal musings, come what may.

Voices of the Wind's Embrace

The wind carries tales from afar,
Whispers of dreams beneath the star.
In its embrace, we find our way,
Voices beckoning through night and day.

Soft sighs rustle through the trees,
Nature's chorus in gentle ease.
Each breath a story, each gust a song,
In the wind's arms, we all belong.

A dance of leaves, a swirling flight,
Guided by the moon's soft light.
The echoes weave through open lands,
Tales of journeys in unseen hands.

Whispers linger in the air,
Secrets of love and tender care.
Through valleys deep and mountains high,
The wind's embrace will never die.

Listen close, let your heart align,
With the cadence of nature's sign.
In the embrace of wind and grace,
We find our voice, our rightful place.

Whispered Reflections in Still Water

In the calm of dawn's embrace,
Ripples dance, a soft trace.
Truths are murmured, shadows play,
In still waters, dreams sway.

Glimmers spark in gentle light,
Secrets held, and taken flight.
A world of whispers waits to hear,
The heart's confessions, crystal clear.

Beneath the surface, stories blend,
Time and memory, a river's bend.
Lost in reflections, I find my way,
The stillness speaks, to night and day.

Each ripple tells a tale untold,
Of fleeting moments, and dreams bold.
In quiet depths, I cast my gaze,
To find myself in the soft haze.

As sunlight breaks, the waters gleam,
Echoes whisper of a dream.
In whispers held, I float and dive,
In still water, I feel alive.

The Shadow of a Thought

Fleeting specter casts a shade,
In the corners, doubts are laid.
An echo softly beckons me,
Whispered truths I cannot see.

In twilight's grasp, reflections stir,
Silent mind, a gentle blur.
A shadow lingers, fades to gold,
Stories buried, secrets old.

Thoughts collide in tangled ways,
Breaking through the misty haze.
A haunting presence, ever near,
Shadows whisper, soft and clear.

In silence, shadows weave their thread,
Guiding where our fears have led.
In every thought, a shadow lays,
A dance of light, through endless days.

Grasping at the ghostly thread,
In my heart, the whispers tread.
Through shadowed realms my mind does roam,
Seeking peace, to call me home.

Whispers Beneath the Moonlight

Underneath the silver glow,
Silent secrets ebb and flow.
Stars above and shadows below,
In moon's embrace, dreams softly grow.

A breeze that sings through ancient trees,
Carrying whispers, sweet as these.
A tapestry of night unfolds,
In whispered tones, the world beholds.

Magic dances on the tide,
Where mysteries and dreams collide.
Every sigh the night enfolds,
With whispered words, the heart consoles.

In the quiet, souls connect,
Under watchful eyes, reflect.
By moonlight's grace, we find our way,
In tender light, shadows play.

As dawn approaches, whispers fade,
Into the light where dreams are laid.
Yet in the heart, those soft tones stay,
Reminders of a night's ballet.

Tidal Waves of Silence

Crashing waves, a quiet roar,
In the deep, silence finds the shore.
Each swell a moment drawn and lost,
A tidal wave, a heavy cost.

Echoes wash in rhythmic flow,
Carrying whispers, high and low.
In every crash, a story brews,
Of silent hopes, of worn-out shoes.

The ocean speaks in hushed tones,
In the void, our longing moans.
Yet in silence, strength resides,
A vast expanse where fate abides.

In the depths where shadows lie,
Secrets linger, and dreams can die.
Yet through the stillness, voices sound,
In every silence, truth is found.

As waves retreat and echoes cease,
A gentle calm brings forth release.
In tidal waves of silence, I stand,
Finding solace in nature's hand.

Notes of an Untold Story

In silent rooms where shadows play,
A tale awaits, lost in the fray.
Whispers drift from page to page,
Unraveling thoughts, our hearts engage.

Beneath the ink, emotions blend,
A fragile thread, where dreams extend.
Each word a marker, secrets hold,
In quiet corners, the past unfolds.

Old photographs, the moments freeze,
Voices echo, carried by the breeze.
Silent wishes that we once penned,
In these notes, our lives transcend.

An open book, with empty spines,
A journey written between the lines.
Each verse a promise, soft and bright,
In every line, a flickering light.

So pause a while, and listen close,
For untold stories matter most.
They guide us through the darkened night,
With every word, our souls take flight.

Gentle Remnants of Time

Softly tracing patterns in sand,
Time slips away, like grains so grand.
Memories linger, whispers of days,
In golden hues, the sunlight plays.

Time's gentle hands paint the skies,
Every sunset, a sweet reprise.
Echoes of laughter, shadows dance,
In fleeting moments, we find our chance.

Old rocking chairs creak with sighs,
Where stories rest, and love never dies.
Windows glow with warmth at dusk,
In every heartbeat, lives we trust.

Leaves fall softly, like gentle tears,
They speak of love, they heal our fears.
Through changing seasons, we learn to see,
Gentle reminders of what can be.

So cherish now, let moments unfold,
In gentle remnants, new tales are told.
Each breath a treasure, a fleeting chime,
In the fabric of our love, there's time.

The Whiff of Longing

In the stillness, a scent so sweet,
A memory lingers, bittersweet.
The whiff of longing, soft and near,
Brings back moments, once held dear.

Beneath the stars, where dreams once bloomed,
In silent nights, our hearts consumed.
Musky petals and rain on stone,
In every breath, the past is sown.

Time drapes softly, like a lover's sigh,
Holding echoes of goodbyes.
Fragrance of promises, lost in dreams,
Woven closely, or so it seems.

With every whisper, a name is called,
In fragrant memories, we are enthralled.
The quiet air, a reminder here,
Of love and loss, of joy and fear.

Yet hope lingers, like springtime's grace,
In the scent of longing, we find our place.
With every breath, we chase the night,
To find the dawn, to seek the light.

A Whisper Through The Trees

Amidst the forest, shadows play,
A whispered secret in the sway.
Leaves rustle softly, like a sigh,
Nature's voice, a gentle cry.

Branches arch as if to speak,
In every rustle, truths unique.
They tell of journeys, stories old,
Of life unspoken, hearts bold.

Sunlight filters, a golden hue,
In emerald canopies, peace renews.
A whisper through the trees we find,
Echoes of love, through space and time.

Roots entwined beneath the ground,
In silent strength, connection found.
Nature's tapestry, rich and vast,
A timeless bond, holding fast.

So wander deep, where silence breathes,
And listen well to what it weaves.
In whispered tales, the heart receives,
A promise held, as nature grieves.